perfectly
imperfect

perfectly imperfect

ATTENTION: SCHOOLS AND BUSINESSES
Dare To Rise Publishing LLC books are available at quantity discounts with bulk purchase for educational, business, or sales promotional use. For information, please email the Dare To Rise Publishing Sales Department: daretorisesales@gmail.com.

perfectly imperfect

A collection of poetry and prose

KELLEY GREEN

Dare To Rise Publishing

DTR

Contents

introduction

i have to be open.
open in a way that heals the hearts of those left broken.

youth lessons

hey pretty girl, don't listen to those little boys—
they weren't raised to know all of God's children are
beautiful.

i wish someone would've told me boys couldn't
and wouldn't define my value.

i looked in the mirror and wondered when my big lips
would curve inward like the
women around me with husbands.
you know, the philtrum, also known as my cupids' bow.
i didn't know it then, but the word philtrum
came from the Greek term meaning "love potion."
it makes sense now, why i wanted it so bad.

everybody else was doing it…
talking about relationships,
talking about sex,
talking about making sure you keep your man in check.
i didn't know what it all meant, so i pretended i did.
we were only in elementary school
but this is what made for elementary discussions.

you were trying to figure out a way to fit in,
searching for a way to feel safe and wanted,
so you led your way to a door labeled "follower."

i listened to her,
like a fool and a follower.
i wanted to grow up so badly.
i just wanted to be like an adult,
since they treated my body like i was one anyway.
without hesitation, she ripped out my handlebar tassels,
to the new bike my dad bought me.
she didn't know she also ripped out my back bone.

is love nothing but pain?

she was awakened by the cries of her
mother that night.
the sound traveled from the bottom of the stairs,
so that's where she ran to.
she saw a tall figure standing there but he
wasn't helping her up.
each shove to her mother's body made her
feel helpless and angry,
but she just stood there. frozen.
feet planted firmly on the carpet.
she learned how to be afraid and silent that night,
when courage was what she was praying for.

you told me you were hurting me
because you love me and had to teach me a lesson.
it should be no surprise that's why i associate
pain with love.

they called each other out their names so much
that you forgot how to say mommy and daddy.

it's amazing how much you
forgive your family for.

take me to the park so i can learn how to be a kid.
i want to feel the wind glide against the curves
of my face.
i want to run,
i want to fall,
i want to find out what it takes to
dare to rise and be strong.
i'm tired of hiding.
i want to learn how to survive.

they told me to be more careful,
they said i had to be less wild.
that i can't be a girl with scars on my legs,
because it doesn't look good.
all i wanted to do was be myself and be free.

you taught me how to swim yet,
these boys still drowned me in my tears, daddy.

i wondered where mine were.
everyone else was getting them—
unclothed looking like a little boy,
i was admiring their figures.
tissues helped but also hurt my ego.

teach our young girls how to love themselves
instead of teaching them how to
find the flaws in others.

they say hands on experiences are the best,
but no one tells you deciphering between
the good and bad examples of your parents,
are the true test.

while you were busy adulting, you forgot us children
were busy lurking.
we picked up on your ways and mimicked your life
when healthy and hazy—
the yelling, the screaming, the cursing, the hurting.
the loving, the pleasing, the hugging, the holding.
it was the times when you forgot we could hear behind
closed doors, was when we learned what love was like
behind closed doors.

but who's going to teach me what love is?

love lessons

you walked by me and i did a double take.
my knees felt weak and they began to shake.
we were freshmen in college but you looked so
grown like a real man.
one that could handle me,
teach me new things,
and take care of me.
i was in awe of you and i couldn't wait for
you to realize that you needed me.

you made it easy for me to love you,
you proved that roses were red and violets were blue,
your actions matched your words and i loved
that i trusted you.

kiss me on my forehead
and tell me how sweet i smell.

you taught me how to love without boundaries.
i felt secure in "us," even when
you weren't around me.

you let me love you
without fearing
i was overdoing it.

you wanted to touch my soul
before touching my body.
i was in awe of you.

he introduced me to a world where love was love.
i was awakened by a real man who worked hard to
earn my trust.
he wasn't focused on lust but he wanted to feed me.
he fed me truths and not lies,
i devoured his every morsel—
mind. soul. and mmm... that body...
my walls had not felt him yet but
i admired all that i had seen.
i was nearly positive, he was the same man
from my dreams.

my dad told me to wait for a man like you.
that i was only worthy of a love that was real and true.

he's the kind of man i used to
write about in my diary.
the type of man i would want
for my daughters.

his energy was electrifying.
he made me feel tingles down my spine and
below my waistline.
i almost couldn't believe this man was all mine,
then i realized i deserved to feel like this...
i deserved a love that was a reflection of excellence.

he planted his seed deep in my heart.
i watered it with his soul and
love buds began to sprout,
just like the flowers that bloom in the springtime.

he pressed his lips on the back of my neck and
called me gorgeous.
he ran the tips of his fingers
down my chest towards my navel.
his strong hands softly grasped the sides of my waist
as i felt him harden against my backside.
he whispered softly in my ear,
"i'm so lucky that you're all mine."

some of these guys have forgotten how to make
phone calls, but not him.
my man knows how to connect with me and said
he loves the sound of my voice.
i wasn't worried about getting sent to voicemail
or getting left on "read" as a choice.

my face was buried in his chest while his hand
rested on my hip—
this was nothing new.
what i didn't expect was for him to say
"baby, i prayed to have a woman like you."
i was his blessing.
he said, "i'll never let you go because i know
God made you just for me."

i love you.
you're the best thing
that ever happened to me.

my legs were straddled around his waist.
he kissed me so deeply, just the way i like it.
i stared into the eyes of the man who i was
into while he was into me.
i let him shoot his stars into my
dark-casted sky so he would brighten it.
i want to see a half of each of us
brought into this world.

he's the type of man who buys me flowers just to
put a smile on my face.
you know, the type of man who you doubt
even exists, while you lay in bed single, and in your
darkened loneliness.
he's the type of man i want to have around and
keep around forever.

he texted me back quickly,
never left me on read,
posted me on his instagram and
tagged me with respect,
asked me to be his girlfriend the
good old fashioned way,
said he didn't want to rush into sex because
he wasn't here to play,
i started to wonder if it was all a dream,
but if it is don't wake me up because this is how
relationships should be.

when i raised my head to feel the warmth of
the sun, i felt God.
when i looked at my man, i felt God too.

i loved watching him stare at me from our reflections—
a mirror, a car window, a wall made of glass.
i would always sneak and watch him.
i watched him smile and inhale me like he was so
grateful i was his.

he made it easy for me to love him.
it was easy to love him deeper than
any pain i've felt before.

we were blessed with the gift of falling in love.
we were bright enough to choose to stay in love.

you held the weight of my past
and comforted it.
judging me was the furthest thing
from your mind.

babe,
remind me to thank
your parents for you.

i sat, legs crossed, on the floor between his legs.
we shared each other's laughter while watching
"Insecure" on HBO.
we were up until 2 am because he was helping me
take out my weave.
blessed be this king because all the while, he was
complaint free.

he was more walk than talk.
his actions were louder than the words that he spoke.
he wasn't playing me nor was he gaming me.
he was the epitome of what love should be.

i hopped in the shower after a long winter day
and shortly after, he joined me.
very swiftly and softly, before i could hesitate,
he grabbed my loofah and squeezed it.
the soap suds ran down my body while
he lathered me up.
the hot water slid down my back
and the heat fogged up the shower door.
i moaned and simultaneously released my exhaustion.
he rinsed us off and stepped out the shower with
his hand extended, so that i could follow him into
our bedroom.
he said, "come on."
i said, "i'll be there in a second, i just want to
shave real quick."
he said, "don't worry about that, i said come on."
he made love to me that night, stubble and all.

he didn't make me feel less than,
i never felt like i wasn't enough.
i was his only target when making a woman blush
and we weren't on the "hush hush."
he claimed me in public,
kept our business private,
fucked my mind really good,
and his love was inviting.
he made me feel safe
but not over protected.
he highlighted my intelligence
and said i was the epitome of black girl magic.

ever met a man with morals?
what about one who loves and listens to God?
how about a man who wanted to get deep inside you
spiritually,
instead of just sexually?
i never did either,
until i met him.

heartbreak lessons

i was a pushover for you,
even after we were through.

there i was,
crawled up in a ball on the floor
with a lump in my throat the size of a lemon.
i hadn't eaten in hours and i was certain
i produced enough tears to water a thousand gardens.
i couldn't believe what you had said to me.
yet, i couldn't find a shovel big enough to dig out
the words that were now buried in my memory:
"i slept with her."
"i slept with her."
"i slept with her."
you forgot to add "and i destroyed you."

we said we would just be friends,
but being each other's friends made us phony
so we became more when we became horny.
it wasn't right but our body's sensations
were stronger than the distance of a nation.
underlying our lies was lust masked as love.
we lied to each other,
we convinced each other we would last,
but no sooner than we spoke of a future,
we became each other's past.

you said you loved me and i believed you—
that was my mistake.

you always got defensive when
i questioned you about claiming me.
i should've realized your only aim was
to make me your side piece.

i had a temper tantrum when you said you were leaving
me for her—
tears, kicks, screams, and you watching me collapse
to your feet couldn't keep you with me.
your heart was already with her.
to make matters worse, i knew her,
i saw her, i met her, we breathed the same air,
and you chose her over me, despite my despair.
how could you not care that you were killing me?
ripping out my heart, soul, and dignity piece by piece.
i can't believe you left me and closed the
door behind you.
hopefully, one day, i'll learn it is a blessing that
we are through.

you were more trick than treat.
like a con artist, you had nothing but
deception up your sleeve.

you said hello and goose bumps
ran down my skin like daisies,
but your soul and skin were no gardens.
they mimicked the souls of men all tarnished.
inside of you was vacant of where a
heart should've been.
and still... i let every part of you in.
like loose lips you sank your ship
into my sea of dreams.
i hoped you'd stay but instead
you came and went like a thief in the night,
clothed not in white but the opposite,
which gave me a fright.
that made me want to pick a fight with you,
pop a tire or two,
spend my life with you—
no wait. how did i still think the best of you
when the truth was you were a mess,
a fool,
and clowns aren't cool so neither are we.
be gone with you and your polygamist mentality.
i'm tired of you,
it's time i do me.

she told him she is not one to
play games with,
except her words fell upon
the ears of a fuckboy.

he promised not to
play games with me.
he lied.

when we first met, my body was his mystery.
but soon it became his history,
which was followed by my misery.
why had i let you enter me?
i was weakened by your sweet talk, light eyes,
and caramel skin.
i thought that if i let you in,
you'd never leave my side again.

i can't remember the last time i fell asleep
without tears in my eyes.
my heart, full of your lies, felt heavy and broken.
i felt lost, confused, used, and unspoken for,
wishing i could've been easier to love and
worthy of being held onto more.

i needed you but you said
she needed you more right now.
there was a calmness in your voice as you explained
to me why you were still texting your ex.
i felt a mess.
i was confused.
i was stressed.
yet, you spoke to me with the aim of
creating understanding.
my reluctance made you feel like
your selfish ways would fumble,
so you told me you was feeling me and asked me
if i knew what that meant.
i became silent.
you said, "it means, i love you."
without hesitation i said, "i love you too."
you succeeded in turning me into a fool.

i was tired of her texting you
so i stole her number from your cell phone.
i texted her "he's with me"
and i watched as she blew up your phone to no avail.
you were smart enough not to answer her while
you were with me.
i was a fool enough to keep you in my company.

i was mad at you
for not being enough for me.

i put my pride aside and i asked my voice
to push past the lump in my throat as i tried to
fight back my tears.
i said, "please don't do this, don't leave me.
i love you."
i can still feel the cold blast of air as the
door shut behind you.

yes, it's true.
i made another mistake—
i did not fall for him.
i fell for the man i wanted him to be.

i tried to make a home out of him.
he tried to make me his vacation house.

he was like a thief in the night,
coming and going when it was convenient.
stealing pieces of me each time,
my love was depleting.

he made me feel like
it was safe to unpack my baggage.
but when i did,
he left me on the floor with the mess.

he taught me that
some of the greatest actors
never make it on stage.
instead,
they find their way into
our relationships.

the greatest lesson you taught me
was teaching me what love is not.

my love is not a revolving door,
you are either in or you're out.

i never knew i could literally feel my heart shatter
into pieces until after you abandoned me.
i did nothing wrong and yet you disrespected me.
you stomped on my heart and you left me bleeding.
your love for me was completely misleading.
you were a fraud and a thief and you left me in pieces.
you left me on my knees crying and trying to
release the pain.
i was trying to convince myself i wasn't going insane.

shh… i'm trying to heal
so please
don't mention
his name.

i needed to
get over you,
even though
i still wanted you.

your presence made me lose my breath.
not in a weak-in-the-knees kind of way.
more like i was high on the swing,
now i've fallen off and got the air knocked out of me.
but you always picked me up and dusted me off.
you were my pain and my remedy.

he said he was different,
but he proved to be no different than the rest.
he said he would be loyal,
but he lured me into royally being screwed, at best.

"i'm sorry."
"i love you."
"i'll never leave you."

these were three of your favorite lies.

he made a liar of himself
and a fool out of me.

somehow,
in the process of learning to love you,
i've learned how to lose myself.

i loved you too quickly and too deeply.
why do i always do that?

you tricked me into trusting you—
your smooth words, full beard, and nice smile
practically made me stupefied.
all i wanted to do was give my all to you,
but you tossed me away like i meant nothing to you.

my loyalty is strong.
i would always look him in his eyes
and i never told him lies.
i, blinded by love,
didn't realize
the man i was talking to was living in a disguise.
he fooled me into loving him and
made me compromise —
i compromised
my morals,
my values,
my self-respect,
and my body.
he was worse than a murderer,
for he aimed to kill my soul.
he knew what he was doing
when he tried to kill the best part of me.

i should've paid more
attention to your energy
and less to your physique.

revival lessons

for every fallen moon,
there will always be a rising sun.

one day my legs regained their strength.
i found the entrance to the exit
and walked out of our relationship.

the tears have run dry,
the heart has begun to heal,
when his name is now mentioned,
there's less pain that i feel.

kelley green

i finally found my happy
without him.

it's surviving the things
that are meant to destroy us,
that makes us more powerful.

kelley green

walk around with a pure heart
and God will make a way for you to have
pure happiness.
trust and believe your time for joy is
already on the way,
because that struggle you're in right now is
only temporary.

i dreamed of you,
i needed you.
you left me,
but i'm a better me,
because of you.

you have survived a breakup.
drop off your "baggage" in the trash,
wipe the past off of your hands,
and prepare for your breakthrough.

you are beautiful
and worthy of receiving
the kind of love you love to give.

sometimes when you think about past relationships,
it's easy to create an image of the time lost,
the passion lost, or the friend that is now a stranger.
it's easy to dwell on the past
but you have to step out of your sadness
and remember that you made no mistake.
God makes no mistakes.
everything happens for a reason
and every move you make,
whether you like it or not,
is a lesson learned.

it's not too late
to be found by someone
who loves you like you want to be loved.

be still,
be quiet,
just rest.
your mind must stop racing
in order for you to be your best.

congratulations,
the day has arrived when you no longer
lose your breath when you think about him.

you are phenomenal
just the way you are.

that boy was just a lesson,
that's why he's no longer around.
he was meant to teach you
what it's not like to be loved by a real man.

you are whole without him,
breathe easy, my dear.
release him.
he can't hurt you anymore.

to him, there was no value in your tears.
losing you was not his fear.
but now that you're no longer there,
he can't eat, sleep, or think straight,
because life without you is hard to bear.

your happiness starts within you.
stop searching for it elsewhere.

he wasn't meant for you,
that's why he had to go.
God needed him to leave
to make room for you to grow.

i was in love with
the picture of you i drew in my mind.
then i erased all the memories of you
from when my love for you was blind.
that was the beginning,
but i've since grown and i've conquered.
i've changed your identity
to the real you in my mind.
that's how i got over you
and i refuse to once again
try to turn back the hands of time.

it's easy to ignore you now—
phone calls,
texts,
and dm's
have no value to me now.

allow faith to be your fuel
as you push past the pain.

you broke me down
but you couldn't keep me down.
you made me frown whenever you were around,
but now i smile wide after all the tears i've cried.
i am blessed i made it out alive.

i feel whole again.
my heart no longer bleeds
from the beating you gave it.
thou shall still remain nameless,
but i am now shameless
because your worth to me
is no longer worthy of sympathy.

it's finally my time to rejoice.
my bed is no longer my place of solace.
i feel free of my love that you once tarnished.
i've learned to love again.

look how far we've come.
this is only the beginning of the rest of our lives,
which is waiting for us.
it's the strength we've acquired
from struggles that were meant to destroy us.
it's what we can carry as we continue
to live powerfully and explore love.

let me remind you,
you are worthy of what you desire.

let down your hair,
walk around the house in your underwear,
eat your favorite snacks and binge watch tv,
do whatever the hell you want because
woman, you are free.

thank you
for teaching me to
never ignore my gut.

self-care has been the savior
of my dark days.
i'm not being selfish
but i'm self-loving me in all my ways.

me settle?
nah. never.

i always knew
you were stronger
than your struggle, beautiful.

finally, i learned the key to
setting the tone in my relationships.
all i had to do was learn to love myself first.

dear self,

i love you

thank you for being here in this moment with me.
this was quite a journey. it took a lot of courage, reflection, acceptance, and resurgence for me to arrive at this page. i am beyond grateful for you and it is emotionally rewarding to know that you are here with me. my hope for you is that in life, you are surrounded by love, guided by positivity, and abundantly favored by your desires. thank you from the bottom of my heart.

xo,

Kelley Green

perfectly imperfect

about the author

Kelley Green is an author, self-love enthusiast, and creative entrepreneur living in Queens, NY. After suffering from the loss of three family members and a spiritual loss of self, she decided to begin her "self-love journey" in 2015. Kelley took to social media and began posting empowering quotes, messages, blogs, and videos of lessons that she's learned while on her journey. This choice of journeying became her therapy and a way to connect with other people who are also struggling as they navigate life, relationships, and their careers. Kelley has expressed her love for "self-love" in many forms and she hopes to continue to express herself and grow as a creative entrepreneur for many years to come.

perfectly imperfect

kelley green

www.ingramcontent.com/pod-product-compliance
Lightning Source LLC
Chambersburg PA
CBHW070518030426
42337CB00035B/4023